AF579069

My Best Bedtime Bible

Text by Sophie Piper
Illustrations copyright © 2011 Claudine Gévry
This edition copyright © 2015 Lion Hudson

The right of Claudine Gévry to be identified as the illustrator of this work has been asserted by her in accordance with the Copyright, Designs and Patents Act 1988.

All rights reserved. No part of this publication may be reproduced or transmitted in any form or by any means, electronic or mechanical, including photocopy, recording, or any information storage and retrieval system, without permission in writing from the publisher.

Published by Lion Children's Books
an imprint of
Lion Hudson plc
Wilkinson House, Jordan Hill Road,
Oxford OX2 8DR, England
www.lionhudson.com/lionchildrens

ISBN 978 0 7459 7608 2

First edition 2011
This edition 2015

A catalogue record for this book is available from the British Library

Printed and bound in China, May 2015, LH17

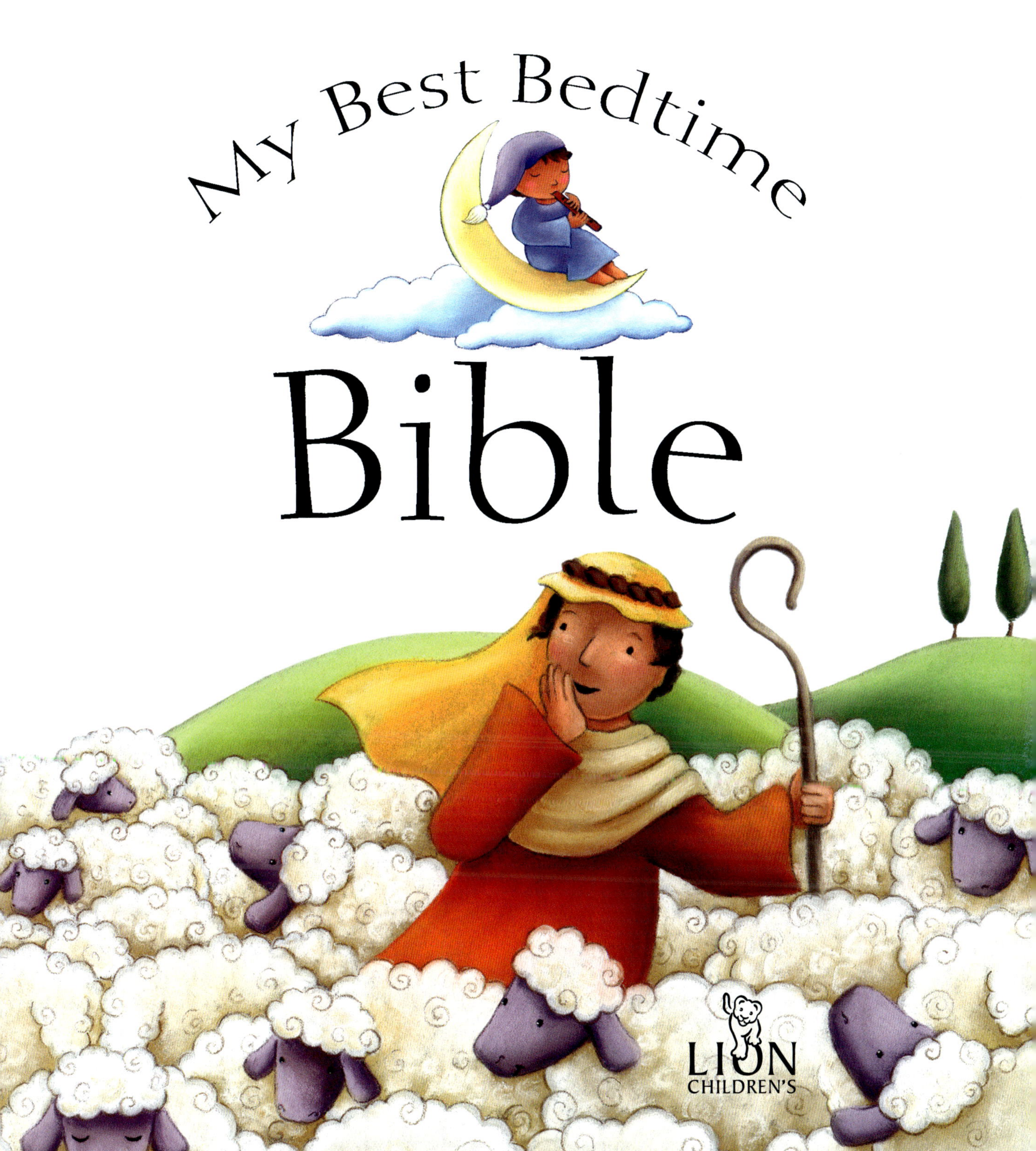
My Best Bedtime
Bible
LION
CHILDREN'S

Who made the world?

Wow!
What a wonderful world.
Long ago, God made the world and everything in it –
the plants, the animals, and people.

When the making was done, God rested.
“Every seventh day is a day of rest,” said God.
“A time to enjoy the world.
“A time to say thank you for all that is good and lovely.”

Thank you, dear God, for the golden sun,
Thank you, dear God, for the day.
Thank you for making a wonderful world –
The world where we live and play.

Thank you, dear God, for the shining stars,
The silvery moon high above.
Now as I lie down to sleep and to dream,
Bless me with goodness and love.

The first rainbow

The raindrops were falling.
“God is sending a flood,” said Noah to his family.
“It will wash away everything that has gone wrong.
“God told me to build an ark.
“We will float on the flood and be safe.
“Me, and you, and all the animals.”

For many days Noah and the animals floated. Day after day after day went by. And still it kept on raining.

At last the flood was over. It was time to begin the world again. The grey clouds blew away. The sun shone. A rainbow spread across the sky.

"I promise," said God, "that there will be summer and winter, seedtime and harvest for ever."

When you see a rainbow
spreading wide across the sky,
know that God takes care of us on earth
from heaven on high.

When you see a rainbow
reaching right down to the ground,
know that you can sleep in peace:
God's love is all around.

Abraham and the night sky

Abraham looked up at the night sky.
Some stars were big and bright. He began to count them.
Other stars were tiny. He stopped counting. There were too many.
Then God spoke. “One day your family will be like that.
“So many great-great-great-great grandchildren! No one will be able to count them all.”

Abraham sighed. “Sarah and I have no children,” he said.
“Will we ever have a son?”
“Yes,” said God. “I promise.”

At long last, Sarah had a baby.
She and Abraham were so happy.
They named the little boy "Isaac". The name means "laughter".
When they looked at the stars, they knew that God's promise had come true.

God who made the sky at night
Keep me always in your sight.

God who made the stars that shine
May your blessings all be mine.

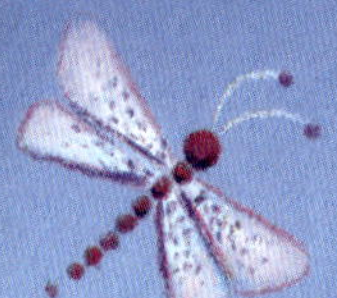

The baby in the basket

Miriam and her mother were in a hurry.
Then the king's soldiers told them to stop.
"We are looking for baby boys," they said.
"The king wants us to throw them in the river."
"I can't see a baby boy," said Miriam. The soldiers marched off.

"It was a good thing we hid my baby brother," said Miriam.
"And we are putting him in the river," said the mother.
"Not throwing… just floating in a cradle."
Miriam stayed to watch.
A princess came down to the river.

The princess saw the basket and the baby.
"I shall keep him safe," she said. "I shall call him 'Moses'."
"I know someone who can help look after him," called Miriam.
She went to get her mother.
Together they kept baby Moses safe.

Keep me safe from every danger
Cradle me throughout the night
Send the angels round about me
Wake me in the morning light.

Jonah and the great big fish

One day, God gave Jonah a job to do.
"Go to Nineveh," said God.
"The people there do bad things. They will soon be in trouble.
"Please go and tell them how to be good."
That made Jonah grumpy.
"Let them be punished," he said.

Jonah hurried off. He got on a boat and sailed away.
"Now you're in trouble," said God to Jonah.
He sent a storm: Jonah sank into the sea.
He sent a fish: it swallowed Jonah whole.
"Help!" said Jonah. "I'm sorry."
God told the fish to take Jonah to shore.

Jonah hurried to Nineveh.
"Listen," he cried. "Stop being bad.
"Start being good."
"Oh dear!" said everyone. "We will."
And God kept them safe.
"Hmmph," said Jonah.
Grumpy Jonah.

Dear God,
Keep me safe through the noisy storm,
keep me safe when I feel afraid.
I know that you love what is good and right
and everything you have made.

Daniel and the lions

In the king's palace, Daniel was saying his prayers.
Some wicked men were watching.
"We can get Daniel into trouble for that," they said.
"Then he won't have his important job anymore."

They went to the king.
“O King! You are great and wonderful,” they said.
“We kneel to you.
“Everyone should kneel to you.
“Anyone who kneels to another should be THROWN TO THE LIONS.”
“I’ll make that a law,” said the king.

The men found Daniel saying his prayers.
"He must go to the lions!" they told the king.
"It's your law."
God sent an angel to the lions' den to keep Daniel safe.
Then the king saw that Daniel's God was great and wonderful.

I know God can hear me
when I say a prayer;
I know God will keep me
safely in his care.

Baby Jesus

In Bethlehem, the inn was full.
The only room for Mary and Joseph was a stable.
There, Mary's baby was born.
She wrapped him snugly and laid him in a manger.

Out on the hillsides, shepherds were watching their sheep.
“Good news!” said the angel.
“A baby has been born in Bethlehem.
“He will bring God’s blessing to the world.
“You will find him lying in a manger.”

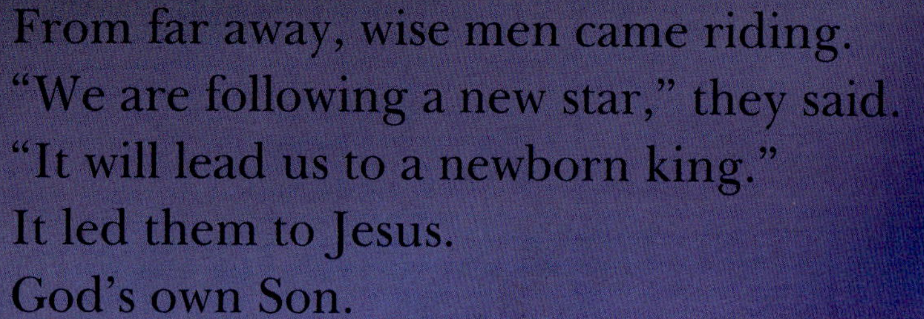

From far away, wise men came riding.
"We are following a new star," they said.
"It will lead us to a newborn king."
It led them to Jesus.
God's own Son.

Little baby Jesus
sleeping through the night:
angels and a new star
filled the sky with light.

Little baby Jesus
sleeping in the hay:
angels bring us safely
to a bright new day.

The boy Jesus

In Jerusalem was a beautiful Temple.
Every year, Mary and Joseph went there for a big festival:
a time to remember God's special love and care.
When Jesus was old enough, he went with them.
So did lots of people from Nazareth.

When the festival was over, they all started out for home.
At the end of the day, Mary went to look for Jesus.
He was lost!
She and Joseph rushed back to find him.
At long last they found him.

He was in the Temple. He was talking with the grown-ups about God's love and care.
"Why did you worry about me?" Jesus asked Mary. "Didn't you know I was in the house of my Father God?"
Even so, he went back home to Nazareth. He was a good son.

God bless all those that I love,
God bless all those that love me,
God bless all those that love those that I love
and all those that love those that love me.

The scary storm

Jesus believed that God was his heavenly Father. When he grew up, he went from place to place telling people of God's love and care.

One evening, Jesus and his friends got on their boat.
He was so tired he fell asleep.
His friends sailed the boat far out on the lake.
Then came a storm: a bad one.
The wind blew, the waves crashed.
“Wake up,” cried Jesus’ friends. “Help us!”

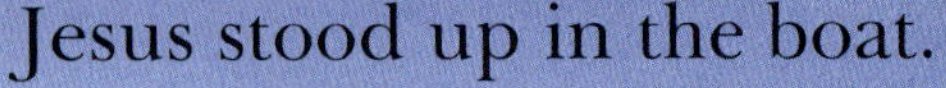

Jesus stood up in the boat.
"Hush!" he said to the wind.
"Lie down!" he said to the waves.
The storm stopped. The lake was still.
"Wow!" whispered his friends. "Jesus is amazing."

Shelter me, dear Father God,
from wind and rain and storm;
may I trust in your great love
to keep me safe and warm.

The lost sheep

"Once there was a shepherd," said Jesus. "He had 100 sheep.
"He cared about them all.
"One day, when he was counting them… oh dear.
"There were only 99.
"He made sure those were all safe.
"He started out to find his lost sheep.

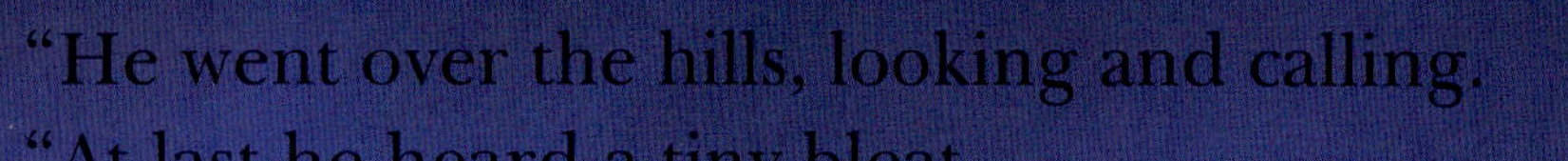

"He went over the hills, looking and calling.
"At last he heard a tiny bleat.
"He hurried to find his lost sheep.
"Gently he picked it up.
"Gently he carried it home.
"God is like that shepherd," said Jesus.
"You are his flock."

When I feel lost and little,
scared and all alone,
may an angel sent by God
come and bring me home.

May I lay me down to sleep
safe in God's great love,
knowing the angels all
are watching from above.